Addressing the Long-Run Budget Deficit: A Comparison of Approaches

Jane G. Gravelle
Senior Specialist in Economic Policy

November 30, 2012

Congressional Research Service

7-5700

www.crs.gov

R41970

Summary

A small share of federal spending is for direct provision of domestic government services, which many people may think of when considering federal spending. Since this spending is normally about 10% of total federal spending and about 2% of GDP and deficits excluding interest are projected to be as much as 7.7% of GDP by 2037, cutting this type of spending can make only a limited contribution. Transfers and payments to persons and state and local governments constitute most of federal spending, about 70%. Defense spending, currently accounting for about 20% of spending, has declined over the past 35 years, but also tends to vary depending, in part, on the presence and magnitude of international conflicts.

Until the recent recession, most types of nondefense spending have been constant or declining as a percentage of output, but spending for the elderly and health care has been rising. Although some increase in the debt can be attributed to the Bush tax cuts and the conflicts in Iraq and Afghanistan, along with growth in spending on the elderly and health care, the current debt level is not the result of prolonged and significant past deficits. Debt grew during the recession and its aftermath. Federal debt held by the public had actually declined from almost 50% of GDP in 1993 to 33% in 2001; it rose slightly to 36% by 2007. During the three recession/recovery years (2008 through 2010), it rose to 62%, and is projected to continue to grow somewhat, before stabilizing for a while. The problem with the debt is due to growth in spending for health care and Social Security if current policies continue. In addition, much of the pressure on future spending arises from imbalances in Social Security and Medicare A (Hospital Insurance) trust funds; thus, keeping these funds and their financing sources intact is an objective that could constrain choices.

Because contributions from discretionary spending appear inadequate to reduce the deficit to a sustainable level, limiting taxes as a percentage of output or constraining the overall size of the government to current levels would likely require significant cuts in mandatory spending, which includes entitlement programs such as Social Security, Medicare, and Medicaid.

Preserving entitlements would eventually require increases in taxes; by one projection the difference between spending on Social Security plus health and taxes leaves less than 2% of GDP for all discretionary and other mandatory spending. Options include allowing the Bush tax cuts to expire, reducing tax expenditures, increasing other taxes, or introducing new revenue sources. Tax expenditures may be difficult to eliminate, but if not used to lower rates they may be a source of additional revenue. Addressing the eventual Social Security trust fund shortfall largely with tax increases would smooth burdens of accommodating longer lives across both working and retirement years. This argument might also apply, in part, to Medicare and Medicaid.

Because the federal government provides about a fifth of the revenue for state and local governments, cutbacks in transfers to these governments may, in part, shift the burden of providing services from the national to subnational governments, rather than altering the overall size of government services.

Contents

Tables

Contacts

Introduction

The growth of the national debt, which is considered unsustainable under current policies, continues to be one of the central issues of domestic federal policy making. On August 2, 2011, Congress adopted, and the President signed, the Budget Control Act (P.L. 112-25), which might be viewed as an initial step in addressing long-run debt issues. A number of tax cuts also expire during the 112th Congress. While it has been recognized for some time that the growing long-term debt is an issue, this concern was reinforced with the downgrading of U.S. Treasury securities by Standard and Poor's from AAA to AA+ on August 5, 2011. More recently, however, short-term concerns about the effect of spending cuts and tax increases on economic recovery have become a central issue for the immediate future.[1]

This report examines alternative approaches to reducing the deficit, relating to the immediate issues arising from the Budget Control Act and the expiring tax cuts as well as to ongoing longer-term decisions about how to bring the debt under control. It focuses on the trade-offs between limiting the provision of defense and domestic public goods, reducing transfers to persons including entitlements for the elderly and those with low income, reducing support for state and local governments, and raising taxes. Using projections of the debt and deficit, it also addresses how limiting reliance on one source of deficit reduction creates pressure on other sources.

The Budget Control Act and Expiring Tax Provisions

The Budget Control Act, the result of months of negotiation, combined an increase in the debt ceiling with proposals to begin reducing the deficit. As a part of legislation increasing the debt ceiling, the Budget Control Act adopted spending cuts with caps that cut discretionary spending by $741 billion from FY2012 to FY2021. Along with mandatory spending reductions of $20 billion and saving in interest of $156 billion, these measures would reduce debt by $916 billion. The agreement also directs a newly created joint committee, composed of 12 members (3 each from the House majority, the House minority, the Senate majority, and the Senate minority) to find an additional $1.2 trillion over 10 years in deficit reduction for a total of 1% of Gross Domestic Product (GDP) over that period from the act.[2] This committee is to vote on a report by November 23, 2011. Members include Democratic Senators Max Baucus, John Kerry, and Patty Murray; Republican Senators Jon Kyl, Rob Portman, and Pat Toomey; Republican Representatives Dave Camp, Jeb Hensarling, and Fred Upton; and Democratic Representatives Xavier Becerra, James E. Clyburn, and Chris Van Hollen. The plan also contained a process and enforcement mechanism.[3] The Committee was unable to reach agreement, setting into motion automatic spending cuts (sequestration).

---

[1] See CRS Report R42700, *The "Fiscal Cliff": Macroeconomic Consequences of Tax Increases and Spending Cuts*, by Jane G. Gravelle for a discussion.

[2] Data on the Budget Control Act from Congressional Budget Office (CBO) letter to the Speaker of the House and majority leader of the Senate, August 1, 2010, http://www.cbo.gov/ftpdocs/123xx/doc12357/ BudgetControlActAug1.pdf. Data on GDP from *The Budget and Economic Outlook, Fiscal Years 2011 -2021*, January 2011, http://www.cbo.gov/ftpdocs/120xx/doc12039/01-26_FY2011Outlook.pdf. Note that CBO scored the committee savings at $1.2 trillion, the amount subject to enforcement mechanisms, although the goal was $1.5 trillion.

[3] See CRS Report RS21519, *Legislative Procedures for Adjusting the Public Debt Limit: A Brief Overview*, by Bill Heniff Jr.

Congress could also reconsider the expiration of the Bush tax cuts, which would increase revenues by slightly more: an increase of 1.5% of GDP through 2014.[4] In addition, at the end of 2012, some other temporary tax cut and expenditure provisions are scheduled to expire, including the 2 percentage point reduction in the payroll tax and some temporary increases in unemployment benefits. These and other proposals that reduce the deficit may, however, be delayed due to concerns about the short run contractionary effect on the economy, popularly referred to as the "fiscal cliff."

The Timing of Deficit Reductions

How much and how quickly to address the budget issues is a topic of some debate. As noted above in relation to the fiscal cliff, there is concern about front-loading deficit reduction at a time when the economy is operating well below potential. Currently, while the economy has stopped contracting from the recent recession, it is growing slowly and unemployment remains high, with current unemployment at around 8%, about three percentage points above the normal 5% in a fully employed economy. (There is always some frictional unemployment.)

Moreover, many of the jobs that have been lost recently are state and local government jobs, and further losses might be contained or avoided with additional transfers to state and local governments. For that reason some believe that the deficit should not be cut until the economy recovers and moves closer to full employment, or that additional spending and tax cuts be considered in the near term.[5] Indeed, although the budget plan agreed upon on August 2, 2011, has limited spending cuts in FY2012, critics of the plan suggested at that time that it might be inappropriate for current economic conditions.[6] Others, however, suggested it did not go far enough.[7] However, the budget plan may be viewed as an initial step toward addressing the long-run budget challenges.

A case can also be made that once the economy has recovered it is important to move quickly to address the deficit, because the greater the debt-to-GDP ratio grows, the more burdensome interest payments become and the more the debt compounds. For example, in the Congressional Budget Office's (CBO's) long-run budget projections, under their alternative baseline, which reflects current services, interest payments rise to 3.7% of output by 2022 and 9.5% by 2037.[8] Delay in addressing the debt also places more of the burden on younger and future generations, which may raise inter-generational equity issues.

The need to not move too slowly can also affect the optimal approaches to deficit reduction. For example, it is difficult to change current entitlements for the elderly (such as Social Security,

---

[4]Data on effect of Bush tax cuts from *The Budget and Economic Outlook, Fiscal Years 2012-2022*, January 2012, http://www.cbo.gov/sites/default/files/cbofiles/attachments/01-31-2012_Outlook.pdf..

[5] Some claims have been made that reducing the deficit could be stimulative in the short run, but this view is inconsistent with mainstream economy theory and the empirical evidence used to support it is problematic. See CRS Report R41849, *Can Contractionary Fiscal Policy Be Expansionary?*, by Jane G. Gravelle and Thomas L. Hungerford.

[6] See Zachary A. Goldfarb, "The Economy: Deal Risks Undermining Fragile Growth," *Washington Post*, August 1, 2011, pp. A1, A7.

[7] Michael A. Fletcher, "Deal Seen by Fiscal Analysts as a Missed Opportunity," *Washington Post*, August 1, 2011, p. A7.

[8] Congressional Budget Office, *The 2012 Long Term Budget Outlook*, June 2012, http://www.cbo.gov/sites/default/files/cbofiles/attachments/06-05-Long-Term_Budget_Outlook_2.pdf.

Medicare and part of Medicaid, which funds nursing home care). Many of those already retired have little leeway to adjust to such changes and could be particularly burdened by benefit reductions, which suggests that benefit changes be adopted in the near term but applicable to the future. Changing discretionary spending or increasing taxes can be achieved more quickly, although, as discussed below, the long-run gap between spending and taxes is too large to be addressed with discretionary spending revisions alone.

Long-Term Budget Issues: Overview

Addressing a federal budget deficit that is unsustainable over the long run involves choices.[9] Fundamentally, the issues involve deciding what government goods and services and transfers are worth paying taxes for (and therefore giving up private consumption). Most people would agree that the country benefits from a wide range of government services—air traffic controllers, border security, courts and corrections, and so forth—provided by the federal government. Yet federal government services, outside of defense, constituted only 10% of federal spending and 2% of GDP in 2007, the last normal year before the recession. Transfers including interest payments account for 70% of the federal budget. Achievable savings through more efficient provision of non-defense federal government services alone would fall short of what is needed to address the deficit.

Transfers including interest payments account for 70% of the federal budget. Outside of the 10% for provision of domestic goods, defense spending constitutes about 20% of federal spending. In this area as well there are limits to the savings that might be found without compromising national security. Therefore to address the budget shortfalls facing the country over the long run, it is likely that transfer payments to or on behalf of individuals (such as Social Security and Medicare), which already account for almost half of federal spending and are growing, must be reduced, transfers to state and local governments must be reduced (which would shift the budget problem to a different level of government), taxes must be raised, or some combination of the above.

The next section of this report examines the allocation of government spending, the method of its financing, and how this has changed over time. It demonstrates that the surge in the debt is a recent phenomenon that has occurred with the recession and is inherently a transitory phenomenon. Going forward, however, as shown in the subsequent section, the growth in transfers to the elderly and for health care, which have been underway for a while but offset by a decline in spending relative to GDP on other purposes, will increasingly contribute to unsustainable deficits. The following section addresses philosophies for approaching deficit reduction, as embodied in a number of proposals. It discusses how different approaches to and constraints imposed on deficit reduction will have consequences for the menus of other choices available. For example, if deficit reduction begins with a constraint that taxes will not rise, policy would almost certainly require significant cutbacks in Social Security and Medicare, while protecting these benefit programs would likely require an increase in taxes.

---

[9] See CRS Report R41784, *Reducing the Budget Deficit: The President's Fiscal Commission and Other Initiatives* , by Mindy R. Levit for a discussion of the issue of sustainability.

Central findings of this analysis include the following:

- A comparatively small share of federal spending is for direct provision of domestic government services, which many people may think of when considering federal spending. Because this spending is normally about 10% of total federal spending and about 2% of GDP, while deficits excluding interest are projected to be as much as 6.6% by 2035, cutting this type of spending alone cannot realistically contain the problem of unsustainable deficits.

- Transfers and payments to persons and state and local governments constitute most of federal spending, about 70%.

- Defense spending, accounting for about 20% of federal spending, has declined as a share of output over the past 35 years, but also tends to vary depending, in part, on the presence and magnitude of international conflicts.

- Until the recent recession, most types of nondefense spending have been constant or declining as a percentage of output, but spending on programs for the elderly and health care have been rising.

- Although some increase in the debt can be attributed to the Bush tax cuts and the conflicts in Iraq and Afghanistan, along with growth in spending on the elderly and health, the concern about the debt is not the result of prolonged and significant past deficits. Debt grew during the recession and its aftermath. Debt held by the public had actually declined from almost 50% of GDP in 1993 to 33% in 2001; it rose slightly to 36% by 2007. During the three recession/recovery years (2008 through 2010), it rose to 62%, and is projected to still grow somewhat, either stabilizing under the standard CBO baseline or growing continually under an alternative baseline that more closely reflects current policies.[10] The problem with the debt lies not in the past, but in the future, as growth in spending for health and Social Security is projected to continue.

- Because much of the pressure on future spending arises from imbalances in Social Security and Medicare A (Hospital Insurance) trust funds, keeping these funds and their source of financing intact is a concern that could constrain choices.

- Because realistic contributions from discretionary spending are insufficient to reduce the deficit to a sustainable level, limiting taxes as a percentage of output or constraining the overall size of the government to current levels would likely require significant cuts in mandatory spending including entitlement programs such as Social Security, Medicare, and Medicaid.

- Preserving entitlements would likely require significant increases in taxes, such as allowing the Bush tax cuts to expire, reducing tax expenditures, increasing other taxes, or introducing new revenue sources. Tax expenditures may be difficult to eliminate, but may be a reasonable source of new revenue if not used to lower rates. Addressing the eventual Social Security trust fund shortfall largely with tax increases would smooth burdens of

---

[10] Debt held by the public excludes intergovernmental debt holdings, such as the debt held by the Social Security trust fund.

accommodating longer lives both across working and retirement years. This argument might apply in part to Medicare and Medicaid issues.

- Because the federal government provides about a fifth of the revenue for state and local governments, cutbacks in transfers to these governments may, in part, shift the burden of providing services from the national to subnational governments, rather than altering the overall size of government services.

Federal Spending and Taxes: Patterns over Time

The objectives of government spending and taxes are generally viewed as providing for public and quasi-public goods,[11] such as defense, law enforcement, infrastructure, and education; correcting market failures,[12] including externalities (both negative, such as pollution, and positive, such as research and development); achieving distributive justice; and managing business cycles. Measured by amount of spending, the most important pure public good the federal government provides is defense. Many public and quasi-public goods, as well as income support programs, are provided by state and local governments, and some of federal spending is through grants to state and local governments. For example, in the state and local governments' fiscal 2007 year, state governments received 21% of total revenues from federal transfers[13] and local governments received 3.6%.[14] States also provide transfers to local governments and local governments provide transfers among themselves as well. These inter-governmental transfers are important in evaluating budget proposals because a reduction in transfers to state and local government may in large part shift the burden to these governments rather than reduce the overall government role.

Spending in the U.S. budget can be divided in a variety of ways that are relevant to considering deficit reduction. In the remainder of this section, government spending is divided by whether the spending is to provide public goods or transfers, whether it is discretionary or mandatory (and the major categories within those divisions), and spending by function. This section also discusses taxes by source, tax structure, tax expenditures, and receipts and payments in the major trust funds.

---

[11] A pure public good is one where there is no marginal cost to an additional consumer. The classic example is a lighthouse, but the most important one in terms of federal spending is national defense. Quasi-public goods do not necessarily have these pure characteristics, but experience large spillover effects. For example, it is possible to charge subscriptions for fire protection, but subscribers benefit from putting out fires in adjacent properties, and allowing a non-subscriber's property to burn is not only generally viewed as unacceptable (especially if lives are at risk) but also endangers other properties and their inhabitants.

[12] A market failure is not the lack of a market but the failure of a market to achieve the optimal outcome where marginal costs equal marginal benefits. Market failures are ubiquitous and many such failures may be too small or too difficult to correct to justify government intervention. Market failures arise from many sources including externalities, monopoly power, imperfect information, and incomplete markets (where contracts cannot be made, such as those between generations). Some kinds of insurance, in particular, tend to suffer from many market failures. A large part of federal government spending relates to insurance against various contingencies, examples being spending on Social Security, unemployment, and health.

[13] See Census data at http://www.census.gov/govs/state/0700usst.html.

[14] See Census data at http://www2.census.gov/govs/estimate/07slsstab2a.xls.

Distribution of Spending By Fundamental Economic Form: Government Goods and Services Versus Transfers

One way to look at spending is to examine the extent to which spending involves actual government consumption/production (that is, spending on the direct provision of goods and services) as compared with transfers. In calendar year 2007, a more normal year than the recent recession years, only 29% of government spending involved the direct provision of goods and services. Of the remaining payments, 45% were transfers to persons, 13% transfers to state and local governments, 11% interest payments, and 2% subsidies.[15] Thus, although federal government spending amounted to 20.6% of output in 2007, spending by the federal government on the provision of public and quasi-public goods was only 6% of output. Based on other budget classifications that indicate discretionary spending on defense is about 4% of output, these numbers indicate that federal government provision for goods and services outside of defense is about 2% of GDP and about 10% of the federal budget. The remainder of domestic discretionary spending, about 1.5% of GDP, consists of transfers to state and local governments.

State and local government spending (netting out transfers between these remaining two levels of government spending) in 2007 was 14% of output, and total spending by all forms of government (after netting out federal transfers) was 32% of output. A larger share of state and local spending, 50%, was in government provision of goods and services (consumption), with 39% transfers to persons, 9% interest payments, and 1% subsidies.

Combining all levels of government, government production of goods and services was 16% of output, so the federal government share (6%) is 38% on the total provided by all levels of government. Subtracting 4% from the federal government share and the total share to eliminate national defense spending, the federal share of non-defense provision of goods and services by all levels of government is 17%.

Similar results are found when examining employment levels. Total government civilian employment is 16% of total non-agricultural employment, with the federal government accounting for 2%, and the state government 4%, with the remainder (11%) local government.[16]

The share of the federal government spending that goes to the direct provision of public or quasi-public goods (consumption) has declined over time as shown in **Table 1**, which compares 1971 to 2007. The year 1971 is used because it is the starting point for CBO historical data. This decline from 9% to 6% of GDP is largely due to a reduction in defense spending, which was higher in 1971 during the Vietnam War.

---

[15] Data in this section from *Economic Report of the President*, 2011, pp. 188, 287-289. Note that numbers may not add up due to rounding.

[16] Ibid., p. 245.

Table 1. Federal Spending by Fundamental Form as a Percentage of GDP, 1971 and 2007

Category	1971	2007
Consumption	9.0	6.0
Transfers to Persons	6.5	9.2
Transfers to State and Local Government	2.1	2.8
Interest	1.6	2.2
Subsidies	0.4	0.3
Total	19.7	20.6

Source: *Economic Report of the President 2011*, p. 289.

The discussion in this section indicates that although total spending as a percentage of GDP grew by about a percentage point, government involvement in the economy, narrowly defined as using resources to provide public goods directly, has fallen by a third, and outside of defense has remained roughly constant and small (at around 2% of output). At the same time, transfers to persons has increased by more than 40% and transfers to state and local governments by more than a third.

Distribution of Spending by Broad Mandatory and Discretionary Categories[17]

Budget accounts often classify spending in budget documents in mandatory and discretionary spending, along with subcategories of spending. Interest payments are listed separately as they are a consequence of past spending and tax policies. Discretionary spending is spending via annual appropriations, and is normally divided into defense and nondefense discretionary spending. It is also sometimes divided into security and non-security spending, although security spending outside of defense is small. Discretionary spending is where most of the public provision of goods and services occurs, although some discretionary spending is in the form of transfers. Mandatory spending is governed by a set of permanent provisions, and some of these programs (such as Social Security and Medicare) are referred to as entitlements. These types of spending are listed in **Table 2** as a percentage of output.

Since 1971, defense spending has declined as a share of output, first as a result of the ending of the Vietnam War (by FY1981, it was 5.2% of output). It rose in the 1980s and then fell, reaching 3.0% by 2001, and rose again with the Afghanistan and (second) Iraq wars. This pattern suggests that while defense spending may generally grow with the economy and be affected by other factors (such as moving to an all voluntary or the peacetime buildup in the 1980s), it also fluctuates depending on whether the United States is engaged in international conflicts.

---

[17] See also CRS Report RL34424, *Trends in Discretionary Spending*, by D. Andrew Austin and Mindy R. Levit.

Table 2. Federal Spending as a Percentage of GDP by Mandatory and Discretionary Categories, FY1971 and FY2007

Category	FY1971	FY2007
Discretionary	11.3	7.5
Defense	7.3	3.9
Nondefense	4.0	3.6
Mandatory	6.7	10.4
Social Security	3.3	4.2
Medicare	0.7	3.1
Medicaid	0.3	1.4
Income Security	1.2	1.5
Other Retirement and Disability	1.3	0.9
Other	1.2	0.7
Offsetting Receipts	-1.3	-1.3
Interest	1.4	1.7
Total	19.5	19.6

Source: Congressional Budget Office (CBO) historical tables, posted at http://www.cbo.gov/ftpdocs/120xx/doc12039/HistoricalTables[1].pdf.

Nondefense discretionary spending has fluctuated much less, although it rose in the late 1970s, then reverted back to historical levels. Nondefense discretionary funding, although small as a share of the budget and of GDP, is the spending that many people think of when they think of government services.

What does nondefense discretionary spending include? About 16% is education, training, employment and social services, and the vast majority of this spending is for elementary and secondary education for disadvantaged and special needs children. A similar share, about 15%, is in transportation, with about half related to highways, almost a quarter air transport, and about one-sixth mass transit, with small shares for marine and railroad. About 11% is for income security (mostly low-income housing assistance); 10% is for health research and public health, 10% for veterans' benefits, 9% for international (about half for humanitarian and development aid and about 15% funding for the State Department); and 9% is for administration of justice (border security, FBI, DEA, courts and corrections). Finally, about 6% is for environment and natural resources (about a quarter of this each being for the EPA and the Army Corps of Engineers, 15% for the forest service, with the remainder for parks, fish and wildlife, and national oceanic and atmospheric programs). About 5% is for general space and science (about half of that for the space program).[18] As noted in the discussion above, it appears that about 40% of total discretionary nondefense spending is for transfers such as highway funds and grants provided to state and local governments.

---

[18] Calculations are based on Congressional Budget Office, *The Budget and Economic Outlook, Fiscal Years 2011 - 2021*, January 2011, http://www.cbo.gov/ftpdocs/120xx/doc12039/01-26_FY2011Outlook.pdf, p. 80, and CRS Report R41783, *A Breakdown or "Receipt" of How Individuals' Federal Taxes Are Spent*, by Margot L. Crandall-Hollick. Note that the CBO numbers are for budgetary authority rather than outlays.

Thus, any one program area is modest as a share of output and cuts in a particular area would also be small. Thus, for example, total spending on the entire federal domestic enforcement program, including immigration and the border patrol, federal courts and prosecutors, federal prisons, and the FBI, constitute only three-tenths of 1% of output, and even a significant cutback is small compared with projected deficits of around 5 percentage points of GDP by FY2021.

Mandatory spending has increased over the period FY1971 through FY2007.[19] The increase is most pronounced for Medicare, which provides health care for the elderly and which has grown relative to GDP due to rising health care costs, certain other benefit changes, aging, and increased life spans. Social Security has also grown relative to GDP, although by a smaller amount, due to aging and longer life expectancy of the population. A large percentage of Medicaid also benefits the elderly (largely through long-term care) and its growth has also been influenced by increased life spans as well as costs. The other mandatory programs that provide benefits for low-income individuals, the unemployed, retirement programs for federal workers, and other purposes (such as agricultural support payments) have remained relatively constant or declined.

Distribution of Spending by Function

Another traditional way of viewing the budget is by budget function relating to the area of spending (education, health, etc.).[20] These comparisons, shown in **Table 3**, provide a similar picture to the previous allocation: although total spending as a share of output has remained about the same from FY1971 to FY2007, the federal government has an increasing share of output in health and programs for the elderly, with declining shares for almost every other functional category. In 2007, 64% of spending was for human resources,[21] with 20% for defense, 9% for interest, and 7% for all other functions. **Table 3** presents these categories as a percentage of GDP, and illustrates that the subcategories for many types of spending, which are those that represent direct provision of government services are small as a percentage of GDP.

---

[19] See CRS Report RL33074, *Mandatory Spending Since 1962*, by D. Andrew Austin and Mindy R. Levit.

[20] See CRS Report R41726, *Discretionary Budget Authority by Subfunction: An Overview*, by D. Andrew Austin, for additional detail.

[21] Further discussion of human resources spending can be found in CRS Report R41827, *FY2012 Budget Highlights for the Human Resources "Superfunction": Education, Training, Social Services, Health, Income Security, and Veterans*, by Karen Spar and Gene Falk.

Table 3. Total Spending by Functional Form as a Percentage of GDP, FY1971 and FY2007

Budget Function	FY1971	FY2007
National Defense	7.3	4.0
Human Resources	8.5	12.7
Education	0.9	0.7
Health	0.6	1.9
Medicare	0.6	2.7
Income Security	2.1	2.6
Social Security	3.3	4.2
Veterans' Benefits	0.9	0.5
Physical Resources	1.7	1.2
Energy	0.1	0.0
Natural Resources/ Environment	0.4	0.3
Commerce and Housing Credit	0.2	0.0
Transportation	0.7	0.7
Community/Regional Development	0.3	0.3
Net Interest	1.3	1.7
Other	1.5	1.0
International Activities	0.4	0.2
General Science and Space	0.4	0.2
Agriculture	0.4	0.1
Administration of Justice	0.1	0.3
General Government	0.2	0.1
Offsetting Receipts	-0.9	-0.6
Total	19.5	19.8

Source: *Budget of the U.S. Government Historical Tables FY2012*, http://www.gpoaccess.gov/usbudget/fy12/pdf/BUDGET-2012-TAB.pdf.

Tax Revenues, Tax Structure, Tax Expenditures and Earmarked Spending

This section discusses four issues related to taxes: the sources of tax revenue and their growth over time, the differences in structure and distribution of revenue sources, the size and distribution of tax expenditures (special income tax provisions such as exclusions, deductions, and credits), and taxes that are specified as the revenue source for certain spending.[22]

---

[22] See CRS Report RL32808, *Overview of the Federal Tax System*, by Molly F. Sherlock and Donald J. Marples, for additional detail on the sources of revenues, their growth over time, and tax structure.

Tax Revenues

Table 4 provides the major sources of revenue and how they have changed over time. The individual income tax, the largest single source of revenue as a percentage of GDP, was about the same in FY1971 and FY2007, but over the time period fluctuated considerably. Individual income tax revenues grew over the 1970s due to bracket creep, reaching 9.4% in FY1981.[23] The tax cuts in the Reagan Administration are the major reason revenues declined, falling to 7.6% in FY1992. Revenues increased slightly with the 1993 Clinton Administration tax increase but the more significant growth occurred with the strong economic performance in the late 1990s, leading to a ratio of 9.7% in FY2001. They declined during the first decade of the 21st century following the George W. Bush Administration tax cuts.[24] Along with the individual income tax, total taxes have also fluctuated, dropping as low as 17.1% in FY1977 and rising as high as 20.6% in FY2001.

Table 4. Revenues as a Percentage of GDP, FY1971 and FY2007

Revenue Type	FY1971	FY2007
Individual Income Tax	8.1	8.4
Corporate Income Tax	2.5	2.7
Payroll Taxes	4.4	6.3
Excise Taxes	1.5	0.5
Estate Taxes	0.3	0.2
Customs	0.2	0.2
Miscellaneous	0.4	0.4
Total	17.3	18.5

Source: CBO historical tables, posted at http://www.cbo.gov/ftpdocs/120xx/doc12039/HistoricalTables[1].pdf.

Corporate taxes have fluctuated as well, although largely due to economic conditions, whereas payroll taxes rose to around their current levels by the mid-1980s, reached a peak of 6.8% in 2001, and have since declined slightly. Excise taxes have declined by a third, and other revenue sources have remained about the same. Part of the decline in excise taxes is because these taxes are imposed on a per unit basis and not indexed for inflation and, with the exception of tobacco taxes, have not been recently increased.

Tax Structure

These revenue sources differ in some important ways. Individual and corporate income taxes are progressive, have graduated rates, and can be revised in a variety of ways including not only changing rates, but also changing deductions, exclusions, and credits. Income taxes are the main source of revenue for most federal spending outside of Social Security and Medicare Hospital Insurance (whose benefits are about half of Medicare spending). Estate taxes are also progressive,

---

[23] Bracket creep refers to the increase in the effective tax rate as nominal income grows because at that time exemptions and rate brackets were not indexed for inflation. There is also some amount of real bracket creep that causes effective tax rates to rise over time as real income grows.

[24] See CRS Report R41393, *The Bush Tax Cuts and the Economy*, by Thomas L. Hungerford, for further discussion.

but are very small, and currently are smaller than in FY2007. Payroll taxes, which are significant, and excise taxes, which are small, tend to fall more heavily on middle- and lower-income individuals.

Payroll taxes, the next largest source of revenues after income taxes, have flat rates with an earnings cap for Social Security (but not Medicare). These taxes tend to be proportional with a reduced burden on high-income taxpayers, and because of their simple structure the main options for increasing revenues from this source are rate increases or raising or eliminating the earnings cap. Social Security taxes are the basic source of finance for Social Security and are linked to benefits so that larger taxes lead eventually to larger benefits, although there are progressive elements in the benefit formula. Medicare payroll taxes qualify individuals for Medicare hospital insurance coverage, but the Medicare benefits are the same for all recipients.

Excise taxes, which largely apply to alcohol, tobacco and transportation fuels, tend to be regressive but are also small. Transportation fuel taxes are a major source of finance for highways, airports, and other transportation needs.

Tax Expenditures

Tax expenditures are revenue losses attributable to federal income tax laws, which allow a special exclusion, exemption, deduction, credit, preferential rate of tax, or a deferral of tax liability. The special tax credits and deductions in the income tax can also be viewed as a form of spending through the tax code. That is, one can view revenues as receipts without the special benefits, and think of the special benefits as spending. In FY2007, without tax expenditures, individual income tax receipts would have been estimated to be 77% larger, corporate receipts 25% larger, and overall income tax receipts 39% larger. According to a GAO study, tax expenditures have tended to be around 7.5% of GDP during the period of their study (FY1974-FY2004). In FY2007, tax expenditures were 7.2% of GDP and about 36% of total government direct spending.[25]

Viewed from the perspective of dividing government activity between transfers and direct provision of public goods, as in **Table 1**, tax expenditures are transfers and subsidies that go to persons, as is the case with the bulk of federal spending. Viewed from the perspective of discretionary versus mandatory spending as in **Table 2**, they are a mandatory form of spending. Finally, viewed from the perspective of budget function, as in **Table 3**, and as shown in **Table 5**, which compares spending and tax expenditures by function for FY2004, the pattern of tax expenditures is quite different from spending. A much larger share of tax expenditures is for physical resources. For specific subcategories, the largest share of tax expenditures is for Commerce and Housing, a category which attracts a small share of spending. The size of this category reflects special benefits for earnings from capital income. It also reflects benefits for housing in the form of mortgage interest and property tax deductions and, to a lesser extent, exemption from capital gains tax on owner-occupied housing and the low-income housing credit. The relatively large share for general government reflects tax exempt bonds and itemized

---

[25] GAO, *Tax Expenditures Represent a Substantial Federal Commitment and Need to be Reviewed*, GAO-05-690, September 2005. http://www.gao.gov/new.items/d05690.pdf. Estimates for tax expenditures for 2007 are from Committee on the Budget, United States Senate, *Tax Expenditures: Compendium of Background Material on Individual Provisions*, December 2006, Senate Committee Print 109-072. Fiscal Year GDP estimates are from Budget of the U.S. Government Historical Tables FY2012, http://www.gpoaccess.gov/usbudget/fy12/pdf/BUDGET-2012-TAB.pdf.

deductions for state and local income and sales taxes. (These amounts could also be distributed across the functional categories of state spending and thus would be more broadly distributed. Much of the benefit for tax exempt bonds goes to education and highways, where funds are borrowed for capital improvements.) Tax expenditures also provide significant benefits for health, through the exemption of employer provided health insurance and for income security, largely through benefits for pensions and other retirement savings.

Table 5. Federal Spending and Tax Expenditures by Function as a Percentage of GDP, FY2004

Budget Function	Spending	Tax Expenditures
National Defense	3.91	0.02
Human Resources	12.75	3.00
Education, Training, Employment, Social Services	0.75	0.11
Health	2.16	1.01
Medicare	2.31	0.24
Income Security	2.96	1.44
Social Security	4.10	0.17
Veterans' Benefits	0.51	0.03
Physical Resources	1.01	2.89
Energy	0.0	0.02
Natural Resources/ Environment	0.26	0.02
Commerce and Housing	0.05	2.80
Transportation	0.55	0.04
Community/Regional Development	0.13	0.02
Net Interest	1.37	0.01
Other	1.56	0.86
International Activities	0.23	0.10
General Science and Space	0.20	0.06
Agriculture	0.13	0.00
Administration of Justice	0.39	0.00
General Government	0.19	0.61
Offsetting Receipts	-0.50	—
Total	19.80	6.78

Source: *Budget of the U.S. Government Historical Tables FY2012,* http://www.gpoaccess.gov/usbudget/fy12/pdf/BUDGET-2012-TAB.pdf; GAO, Tax Expenditures Represent a Substantial Federal Commitment and Need to be Reviewed, GAO-05-690, September 2005. http://www.gao.gov/new.items/d05690.pdf.

Note: The refundable portions of provisions such as the earned income credit are not included in tax expenditures. These effects are small.

Earmarked Revenues and Trust Funds

As noted above, spending on some categories of services is financed by dedicated revenues, some of them termed trust funds and some special federal funds. There are about 200 trust funds but only a handful are important in magnitude or for considering budgetary reform.[26]

In some cases, the trust funds lead to important questions about addressing the deficit. Although some of these funds rely on contributions from general revenues, the Social Security and the Medicare Hospital Insurance (HI) trust funds rely on payroll taxes. (Transfers are made to the Social Security and Medicare HI trust funds in the amount of income taxes collected on Social Security benefits. A temporary transfer is also being made for the temporary 2% point reduction in the employee share of Social Security taxes for 2011.) The largest trust funds relate to Social Security, which is divided into Old Age and Survivors Insurance (OASI) and Disability Insurance (DI), and Medicare, which is divided into Hospital Insurance Part A and Supplemental Medical Insurance (SMI), Parts B and D.[27]

Payroll taxes are the basic source of finance for Social Security and Medicare HI (also known as Medicare A). These programs are organized through trust funds that can also hold assets and earn interest. Medicare Supplemental Insurance to pay physicians and drugs is financed by a combination of premiums and general revenues.

Table 6 shows the inflow of revenues and the payment of benefits in the three trust funds financed by payroll taxes. (This table does not include earnings from interest on government securities held by the funds and transfers of income taxes collected on Social Security benefits; it also does not reflect administrative costs.) As indicated in the table, in the HI fund, benefits exceeded taxes in FY2007 and the Social Security trust funds were close to or at the point where payouts were as large as revenues. Because initial Social Security benefits are indexed to wages (and subsequently to prices), they tend to be a relatively constant share of output. Benefits have also grown because of increasing longevity. Revenues also tend to be a relatively constant share of output, but were increased in the mid-1980s. Medicare as a program expanded significantly in its scope as well during this period.

Table 6. Financing and Benefits in the Social Security and Medicare Hospital Insurance Trust Funds, FY1971 and FY2007

Program	Payroll Taxes FY1971	Payroll Taxes FY2007	Benefits FY1971	Benefits FY2007
OASI	2.9	3.9	2.9	3.5
DI	0.4	0.7	0.3	0.7
HI	0.4	1.3	0.4	1.5

---

[26] See CRS Report R41328, *Federal Trust Funds and the Budget*, by Thomas L. Hungerford for a further discussion. The twelve largest trust funds are Social Security (including Old-Age and Survivors Insurance (OASI)) and Disability Insurance (DI)), Medicare (including Supplementary Medical Insurance (SMI) and Hospital Insurance (HI)), Civil Service Retirement and Disability, Military Retirement, Unemployment Insurance, Highway, Federal Employees Health Benefits, Foreign Military Sales, Airport and Airway, and Railroad Retirement. See CRS Report R41815, *Overview of the Federal Debt*, by D. Andrew Austin, for the amount of federal securities held by various trust funds.

[27] See CRS Report RL33028, *Social Security: The Trust Fund*, by Dawn Nuschler and Gary Sidor, and CRS Report R41436, *Medicare Financing*, by Patricia A. Davis, for further details on the history of these programs.

Note: This table does not show the period beginning in the mid-1980s when sizeable surplus revenues were collected for Social Security.

Table 7 provides income and outflow for the SMI trust fund. In FY1971, this fund was about equally financed by premiums paid by the beneficiaries and federal contributions from general revenues, but, although premiums have increased as a percentage of output, the vast majority of financing is now from general revenues. Although the premium share for Medicare B (physicians) fluctuated over time, it is now set at 25% of the cost; it is not as large a share for the recently enacted Medicare D (drug) program.[28]

Table 7. Income and Outflow as a Percentage of GDP, Supplemental Medical Insurance Trust Fund, FY1971 and FY2007

Income or Outflow	FY1971	FY2007
Premiums	0.1	0.3
Federal Contribution	0.1	1.3
Benefits	0.2	1.7

As these tables indicate, the size of these programs, particularly Medicare, has grown over time. Medicare Supplemental Insurance has grown faster than Hospital Insurance, while the contribution of general revenues has grown at a similar pace. Medicare Supplemental Insurance is currently slightly over half the cost of Medicare.

One open question surrounding the formulation of a long-run budget policy is whether to maintain the financing of Social Security and Medicare HI from payroll taxes. In both cases the benefits due from these programs are expected to outstrip the receipts and eventually draw down all the assets. The Social Security trust fund is projected to run out of accumulated assets in 2036[29] and the HI trust fund in 2024.[30]

In the case of Social Security, there is a long history (dating from 1935 when the program was implemented) of treating the Social Security program as a separate program similar to a retirement plan, in which contributions during the working years create an entitlement to benefits in old age. A similar approach has been used for the more recent Medicare HI. If these programs are to be kept separate, then they will have to be brought into balance separately, and, to maintain the historic source of financing, any shortfall not addressed through benefit cuts or delayed eligibility will need to be achieved through increases in a specific tax, the payroll tax.

---

[28] See CRS Report R41436, *Medicare Financing*, by Patricia A. Davis.

[29] See CRS Report RL33028, *Social Security: The Trust Fund*, by Dawn Nuschler and Gary Sidor, for additional discussion.

[30] See CRS Report R41436, *Medicare Financing*, by Patricia A. Davis for additional discussion.

Growth in the Debt in Recent Years and the Recession

In 2001, the CBO baseline projected a surplus for the next 10 years of $5.6 trillion, which would have led to a further decline in the debt. Ultimately that surplus became a deficit of $6.2 trillion, or an $11.8 trillion shift. Some have addressed the causes of the growth in debt by referring to the shift in these CBO projections. Legislated changes in revenues accounted for an estimated 24% of the discrepancy, with most of that amount reflecting the 2001-2003 Bush tax cuts and extensions of these cuts. 37% reflected changes in spending (with about two-thirds due to discretionary spending), 11% was from increased interest, and the remainder was essentially some form of forecasting error.[31]

The CBO baseline should not be taken as a projection of what future deficits are likely to be for a continuation of current services. Rather, it is a particular benchmark for policy debates that is arbitrary in some ways.[32] For those items (revenues and mandatory spending) that are based on laws other than appropriations, the baseline reflects those laws. Because of that convention, in 2001 the baseline did not allow for some expected tax cuts (such as the indexing of the alternative minimum tax exemption and the extension of temporary tax provisions). On the spending side, the baseline projects discretionary spending as growing with inflation, but not, as historically has been the case, with output. (The purpose of this discussion is not to criticize the baseline, which is constructed to be helpful for policy-making purposes in many ways, but rather to stress what that baseline means.)

It is instructive to consider the path of debt and spending relative to output.[33] In FY1971, debt held by the public was 28% of output, and it fluctuated in that vicinity (as both spending and taxes increased as a percentage of GDP) until the early 1980s. At that point, debt began to rise, reflecting a combination of the recession, lower income taxes, lower spending on nondefense discretionary programs, and higher defense spending. By FY1993, debt held by the public had reached 49.3% of GDP, but following the 1993 tax increase, spending caps, and the strong economic growth in the late 1990s, it declined, reaching 32.5% by FY2001. During this time, there was a gradual increase in health spending (Medicare and Medicaid) and Social Security benefits.

Rather than a decline in the debt after 2001 as would have occurred with a surplus, debt began to rise slightly reaching 36.9% in FY2005, although declining to 36.2% by FY2007. The largest contributor to this rise was the decline in income tax revenues (due largely to the 2001 and 2003 tax cuts and their speed-ups) along with an increase in defense spending and, to a lesser extent, an increase in Medicare payments. (Part of the reason Medicare rose was due to increased payments to physicians. Legislation was adopted in 1997 to limit these payments, the Sustainable Growth Rate [SGR] System, but the cuts required by this legislation have repeatedly been suspended.

---

[31] See Congressional Budget Office, *Changes in CBO's Baseline Projections Since January 2001*, May 12, 2011, http://www.cbo.gov/ftpdocs/121xx/doc12187/ChangesBaselineProjections.pdf. For more detail, see CRS Report R41134, *The Impact of Major Legislation on Budget Deficits: 2001 to 2010*, by Marc Labonte and Margot L. Crandall-Hollick.

[32] The Congressional Budget Office clearly acknowledges caveats surrounding the baseline. See p. xiv of *The Budget and Economic Outlook, Fiscal Years 2011-2021*, January 2011, http://www.cbo.gov/ftpdocs/120xx/doc12039/01-26_FY2011Outlook.pdf.

[33] Data from CBO historical tables, http://www.cbo.gov/ftpdocs/120xx/doc12039/HistoricalTables[1].pdf . See also CRS Report RL34712, *The Federal Debt: An Analysis of Movements from World War II to the Present*, by Mindy R. Levit.

Addressing the increased spending compared with the baseline in reference to deficit reduction proposals is referred to as the "doc fix.")[34]

This modest increase in debt accelerated with the recession, rising to 40.3%, 53.5%, and 62.1% in 2008, 2009, and 2010 respectively. [35] As shown in **Table 8** and **Table 9**, spending increased and revenues declined during this serious recession, both contributing about equally to the deficit increase by 2010. The increased deficit between these years reflects measures undertaken to combat the recession, along with automatic stabilizer effects (taxes fall and spending rises automatically during a downturn) that increased the deficit by about 2.5% of output between FY2007 and FY2010. (Note that comparing the two years obscures the temporary effect of the Troubled Asset Relief Program; in FY2009, other mandatory spending was 2.6% of output due to this provision, although there was an offset in FY2010, with the net effect small.) On the spending side the increases came from income support programs as well as discretionary domestic spending (defense spending was unrelated), while on the tax side the primary decrease was in income taxes. These effects reflected stimulus provided through tax cuts as well as increases in programs such as unemployment compensation, transfers to states to fund infrastructure, Medicaid, education, and other programs (see **Table 8** and **Table 9**).

The current level of the debt thus accumulated quickly due to the recession and prior to that point was not out of line with historical levels for the past 40 years. That is, what we see today has not been the consequence of years of excessive deficits. Rather, the current debt level reflects years of modest deficits with an increase due to the recession. The next section suggests that current debt problems are less troubling than those projected in the future, arising from population aging and rising health costs. These longer-run spending increases have long been anticipated. In that context, the fact that the U.S. government is beginning from a higher level of debt in the context of a fragile economy (rather than the lower level that was expected in the beginning of the 21st century) makes these future issues more challenging.

---

[34] See CRS Report R40907, *Medicare Physician Payment Updates and the Sustainable Growth Rate (SGR) System*, by Jim Hahn and Janemarie Mulvey.

[35] For a review of developments in the recession and recovery see CRS Report R41578, *Unemployment: Issues in the 113th Congress*, by Jane G. Gravelle, Thomas L. Hungerford, and Linda Levine.

Table 8. Spending as a Percentage of GDP, FY2007 and FY2010

Category	FY2007	FY2010
Discretionary	7.3	9.3
Defense	3.9	4.7
Nondefense	3.6	4.5
Mandatory	10.4	13.1
Social Security	4.2	4.8
Medicare	3.1	3.6
Medicaid	1.4	1.9
Income Security	1.5	3.0
Other Retirement and Disability	0.9	1.0
Other	0.7	0.2
Offsetting Receipts	-1.3	-1.3
Interest	1.7	1.4
Total	19.6	23.8

Source: CBO historical tables, posted at http://www.cbo.gov/ftpdocs/120xx/doc12039/HistoricalTables[1].pdf.

Table 9. Revenues as a Percentage of GDP, FY2007 and FY2010

Revenue Type	FY2007	FY2010
Individual Income Tax	8.4	6.2
Corporate Income Tax	2.7	1.3
Payroll Taxes	6.3	6.0
Excise Taxes	0.5	0.5
Estate Taxes	0.2	0.2
Customs	0.2	0.2
Miscellaneous	0.4	0.7
Total	18.5	14.9

Source: CBO historical tables, posted at http://www.cbo.gov/ftpdocs/120xx/doc12039/HistoricalTables[1].pdf.

Deficit Challenges Going Forward

The CBO baseline projects the debt will grow to about 75% of GDP (around FY2013) and stay in that vicinity through FY2022. (Offsetting debt with financial assets such as TARP funds makes the net debt a few percentage points smaller.) However, CBO also uses an alternative baseline that may reflect policies consistent with current service levels, expectations, or history. In this baseline, the debt will continue to rise through 2021 and will exceed 100% of GDP. This alternative baseline includes discretionary spending rising with output, a continuation of the Bush tax cuts and other tax revisions, allowing Medicare payments to doctors to rise, and some other changes.[36]

Table 10 shows the projected spending against the CBO baseline through 2022. As indicated earlier with respect to the baseline issues, this table includes the effects of spending caps.

**Table 10. Spending as a Percentage of GDP in FY2011 and FY2021:
CBO Baseline Forecast**

Category	FY2011	FY2022
Discretionary	9.0	5.6
Defense	4.7	3.0
Nondefense	4.3	2.6
Mandatory	13.5	14.3
Social Security	4.8	5.5
Medicare	3.7	4.2
Medicaid	1.8	2.5
Other	4.4	3.4
Offsetting Receipts	-1.3	-1.3
Interest	1.5	3.3
Total	24.1	22.4

Source: *The Budget and Economic Outlook, Fiscal Years 2011 -2021*, January 2011, http://www.cbo.gov/ftpdocs/120xx/doc12039/01-26_FY2011Outlook.pdf.

The table indicates that past patterns are expected to continue, in that programs for the elderly and health programs are becoming more costly over time. In addition, as deficits continue and interest rates rise, interest payments will rise as well.

Table 11 shows the forecast for revenues, again using the baseline assumptions that the Bush tax cuts will expire and no further temporary changes will be made (including the temporary reduction in the payroll tax). With these assumptions and economic growth, revenues will rise to almost 21% of GDP by FY2021.

---

[36] See CBO's *2011 Long Term Budget Outlook*, June 2011, http://www.cbo.gov/ftpdocs/122xx/doc12212/06-21-Long-Term_Budget_Outlook.pdf.

**Table 11. Revenue as a Percentage of GDP, FY2011 and FY2022:
Baseline CBO Forecast**

Revenue Type	FY2011	FY2022
Individual Income Tax	7.3	11.5
Corporate Income Tax	1.3	1.9
Payroll Taxes	5.5	6.1
Excise Taxes	0.5	0.5
Estate Taxes	0.0	0.3
Customs	0.2	0.2
Miscellaneous	0.1	0.3
Total	15.4	20.8

Source: *The Budget and Economic Outlook, Fiscal Years 2011-2021, January 2012*, http://www.cbo.gov/sites/default/files/cbofiles/attachments/01-31-2012_Outlook.pdf.

CBO's long-run budget analysis indicates the possible pressures from a more realistic baseline, especially for health programs. **Table 12** and **Table 13** respectively show spending and revenues, along with debt-to-output ratios further into the future under the CBO baseline and under an alternative baseline. This alternative baseline may be more realistic as a representation of current policy.

In both baselines, the rise in transfers for old age and health programs continues while other programs decline in relative size. This rise in health program costs is particularly pronounced under the alternative baseline, where the total of Medicare, Medicaid, and the health programs rise from 5.4% of output to 10.4%. This scenario assumes that Medicare payments to doctors (the "doc fix") will be unconstrained and that other provisions to keep health care spending in check will not occur. In both scenarios, Social Security payments also continue to rise.

The standard baseline assumes that the Bush and other tax cuts expire and income taxes continue to rise through real bracket creep, while in the alternative baseline these tax cuts and others are retained and cuts continue to restrain bracket creep, so that revenues return to FY2007 levels.

Debt to GDP rises in both scenarios, but rises dramatically in the alternative baseline, in which the deficit reaches 17.2% of GDP in FY2037 and the primary deficit (excluding interest) reaches 7.7%. In addition, these scenarios omit the economic effects, which would increase debt as a percentage of output to as much as 250% as the economy contracts under the alternative baseline.

**Table 12. Long-Run Spending, Revenue, and Debt as a Percentage of GDP,
FY2022 and FY2037: CBO Standard Baseline Forecast**

Category	FY2012	FY2022	FY2037
Social Security	5.0	5.4	6.2
Medicare	3.7	4.2	6.0
Medicaid, CHIP, Exchanges	1.7	3.0	3.6
Other Spending	11.6	7.3	6.9
Interest	1.4	2.5	2.7
Total Spending	23.4	22.4	25.3
Revenues	15.8	21.2	23.7
Debt	73	61	53

Source: *CBO's 2012 Long Term Budget Outlook*, June 2012, http://www.cbo.gov/sites/default/files/cbofiles/
attachments/06-05-Long-Term_Budget_Outlook_2.pdf.

**Table 13. Long-Run Spending, Revenue, and Debt as a Percentage of GDP,
FY2022 and FY2037: CBO Alternative Baseline Forecast**

Category	FY2012	FY2022	FY2037
Social Security	5.0	5.4	6.2
Medicare	3.7	4.5	6.7
Medicaid, CHIP, Exchanges	1.7	3.0	3.7
Other Spending	11.6	7.8	9.6
Interest	1.4	3.7	9.5
Total Spending	23.4	24.3	35.7
Revenues	15.7	18.5	18.5
Debt	73	93	199

Source: *CBO's 2012 Long Term Budget Outlook*, June 2012, http://www.cbo.gov/sites/default/files/cbofiles/
attachments/06-05-Long-Term_Budget_Outlook_2.pdf.

Debt Reduction Approaches and Strategies

Numerous proposals have been put forward to address the budget deficit. The Committee for a
Responsible Federal Budget (CRFB) has identified 32 different proposals and provided
comparisons of provisions. This section relies in part on that comparison to summarize the
different approaches taken by the various plans, which provide examples of potential policies.[37]

---

[37] The Committee for a Responsible Federal Budget, Deficit Reduction Comparison Tool, available at http://crfb.org/
compare/index.php?id=01. For a closer look at selected proposals, see CRS Report R41784, *Reducing the Budget
Deficit: The President's Fiscal Commission and Other Initiatives* , by Mindy R. Levit. For additional discussion of
options, see Division of Behavioral and Social Sciences and Education, National Research Council and National
Academy of Public Administration, Committee on the Fiscal Future of the United States, *Choosing the Nation's Fiscal
Future,* National Academies Press, Washington, DC 2010, co-chaired by John Palmer and Rudy Penner,
(continued...)

Although all of the plans aim at reducing the debt-to-GDP ratio, they vary in spending, taxes, and the deficit relative to output. For those plans in which measures are reported (for 2020), spending-to-GDP ratios range from 18% to 25%, whereas taxes-to -GDP ratios vary from 18% to 22.5%. Deficits range from 0% to 4% of output.

Note that a debt level can still be sustainable with some continuing deficit. The deficit causes the debt to grow, but as long as it is not large enough to cause growth faster than GDP, the debt-to-GDP ratio can be stable or declining.[38]

Although summarizing all of these plans is beyond the scope of this report, **Table 14** shows five plans that have been widely discussed along with the CBO standard baseline projection and the CRFB's own projection of what they consider a realistic projection.[39] That projection is similar to CBO's baseline for spending but reflects a tax assumption that permanently extends the Bush tax cuts (similar to the CBO alternative baseline). The five plans are the House Republican Budget Plan, the President's Framework, the bi-partisan government Fiscal Commission, and two private plans that are widely discussed, the Galston-MacGuineas plan and the Debt Reduction Task Force (Domenici-Rivlin). (In subsequent plan comparisons, the Senate's "Gang of Six" plan is also discussed;[40] the CRFB reports no numbers for that plan.) [41]

Most of these plans have spending rise constant or rising relative to 2007 (at which time spending was approximately 20% of GDP) but falling relative to current law (and the CBO alternative baseline) projections. Taxes relative to GDP range from slightly below the 2007 level of 18.5% to slightly above the CBO baseline projection of 20.0% (a baseline that has the Bush tax cuts and other temporary provisions expiring as scheduled).

(...continued)

http://www.ourfiscalfuture.org/wp-content/uploads/fiscalfuture_full_report.pdf.

[38] Specifically, a deficit that remains at the GDP growth rate times the ratio of debt to GDP would maintain a steady state growth. For example, if the debt is 70% of output and GDP grows at 5%, a deficit of 3.5% (5% times 0.7) will maintain a constant debt to GDP ratio. The primary deficit (deficit without interest) will be smaller and could require a surplus, depending on the relationship between the interest rate and the growth rate. The primary sustainable deficit is the ratio of debt to GDP times the growth rate minus the interest rate.

[39] See also The National Commission on Fiscal Responsibility and Reform, *The Moment of Truth*, December 2010, http://www.fiscalcommission.gov/sites/fiscalcommission.gov/files/documents/TheMomentofTruth12_1_2010.pdf; House Committee on the Budget, The Path to Prosperity, April 5, 2011, http://budget.house.gov/UploadedFiles/ PathToProsperityFY2012.pdf; President's Framework for Shared Prosperity and Shared Fiscal Responsibility, April 13, 2011, http://www.whitehouse.gov/the-press-office/2011/04/13/fact-sheet-presidents-framework-shared-prosperity-and-shared-fiscal-resp; Bill Galston and Maya MacGuineas, *The Future is Now*, September 2010, http://crfb.org/sites/ default/files/Galston-MacGuineas_Plan.pdf The Debt Reduction Task Force, *Restoring America's Future*, November, 2010, http://www.bipartisanpolicy.org/sites/default/files/ BPC%20FINAL%20REPORT%20FOR%20PRINTER%2002%2028%2011.pdf.

[40] Senators Saxby Chambliss, Tom Coburn, Kent Conrad, Mike Crapo, Dick Durbin, and Mark Warner, *A Bipartisan Plan to Reduce Our Nation's Deficit*, http://www.kaiserhealthnews.org/~/media/Files/2011/ A%20BIPARTISAN%20PLAN%20TO%20REDUCE%20OUR%20NATIONS%20DEFICITS.PDF.

[41] See also CRS Report R41784, *Reducing the Budget Deficit: The President's Fiscal Commission and Other Initiatives*, by Mindy R. Levit, which compares several plans.

Table 14. Projected Economic Effects of Alternative Budget Plans as a Percentage of GDP

	Spending 2020	Revenue 2020	Debt 2020	Debt 2035
CBO Projection	24.0	20.5	76	96
Committee For a Responsible Federal Budget Projection	24.0	18.5	89	150
Fiscal Commission	22.0	20.5	65	40
House Republican Budget Plan	20.0	18.0	70	48
President's Framework	22.5	19.5	76	
Galston-MacGuineas Plan	22.0	21.5	60	
Debt Reduction Task Force (Domenici-Rivlin)	23.0	21.5	60	52

Source: The Committee for a Responsible Federal Budget, Deficit Reduction Comparison Tool. http://crfb.org/compare/index.php?id=01.

Note: The House Republican Budget Plan was proposed by the chairman of the House Budget Committee and only adopted in part by the House.

In using these proposals to consider approaches, five issues are considered. First, although discretionary spending cuts are the short term target of many proposals, including those currently under consideration, how easy is it to make these specific cuts? Second, to what extent do proposals appear to maintain the current trust fund revenues for Social Security and Medicare and how important is maintaining this relationship? Third, what spending measures would be required, and how realistic might it be, to maintain tax revenues at or below the levels experienced prior to the recessions? Fourth, is there a feasible way to preserve entitlement programs for the elderly and persons with low income (Social Security, Medicare, and low income programs) and what measures would be necessary to achieve that purpose? Fifth, what are the consequences for state and local governments?

How Much Can Discretionary Spending Cuts Contribute?

As indicated in the historical analysis, discretionary spending, whether for defense or nondefense purposes, is not the cause of the long run growth in spending and historically has been relatively constant or declining as a percentage of GDP. Discretionary spending is, however, targeted as a source of budget savings in the proposals and, because it is easier to change in the short run, may be a source of initial savings. Defense discretionary spending has been declining over some time and nondefense discretionary spending will be at a low point (compared with the period FY1971-present) as a percentage of output in the CBO baseline by FY2021.

The CBO baseline already builds in a decline in discretionary spending as a percentage of output because that baseline assumes spending grows at the rate of inflation. There is no magic number indicating how high this spending should be in relation to output. Nevertheless, recent history has indicated that nondefense discretionary spending has been higher in the past and hence cuts will lead to lower level of government services than has traditionally been the case. (Defense spending, as noted above, fluctuates depending on international conflicts, although it has also been increased to respond to perceived threats or other changes such as an all-volunteer force.)

As shown in **Table 15** and **Table 16**, all of the proposals envision a reduction relative to GDP in discretionary spending of both types. [42] At the same time, most of the proposals do not spell out the exact cuts proposed, an important issue given the diversity in nondefense spending, but rather have a general requirement to reduce spending by a fixed amount. That is, these plans generally direct the government and agencies to cut spending without outlining the specifics. Thus, the plans do not indicate, for example, if fewer prisons will exist, if grants for special needs children will be reduced, if fewer highways will be built or repaired, etc. [43] However, one can anticipate these reductions might be significant. For example, the fiscal commission proposed cuts that are 18% below the CBO baseline (as shown in **Table 16.**), which is already at a historically low level by FY2021.

Even so, it is unlikely that discretionary spending can close much of the long run deficit gap. The Fiscal Commission cut, for example, would reduce overall spending by about 1.3 percentage points of GDP. Yet, as seen in **Table 13**, even if interest payments could be held at the same level as in FY2021, the gap between spending and taxes by FY2035 if present policies continue is still more than 9 percentage points. Thus, closing this gap is likely to require cuts in other spending, including entitlements, increases in tax revenues, or a combination.

CBO's budget options contain some specific proposals for cuts in discretionary spending, although most of these are small. [44] For example, consider education, training, employment and social services, the largest category in domestic discretionary spending. CBO includes proposals to eliminate grants for educational opportunities outside school hours for low income students, to limit the availability of grants for college to the neediest students, to eliminate national community service funding (which funds AmeriCorps and similar operations), to eliminate funding for community service jobs for low-income individuals over the age of 55, and to cut funding for the arts by 25%. Taken together, these changes together add up to about $40 billion. In contrast, the Fiscal Commission's cuts appear to be over $100 billion if allocated proportionally to all programs.

Table 15. Defense Spending Proposals in Various Plans

Plan	Provision
CBO Projection	Defense and war spending grows with inflation.
Committee For a Responsible Federal Budget Projection	Base defense grows with inflation, war spending declines.
Fiscal Commission	Defense spending at 2008 levels by 2013; grows at half the rate of inflation.

---

[42] For defense spending some proposals simply propose across the board spending but some proposed specific cuts. Two proposals refer to the President's 2012 budget proposals, which include some specific savings in personnel and operations along with savings in health care, posted at http://www.gpoaccess.gov/usbudget/fy12/pdf/BUDGET-2012-BUD-7.pdf. CBO's budget options include some specific proposals although most indicate small savings; the largest is a proposal for scaling back costs for health care of military personnel and their families. See Congressional Budget Office, *Reducing the Deficit: Spending and Revenue Options*, March 2011, http://www.cbo.gov/ftpdocs/120xx/doc12085/03-10-ReducingTheDeficit.pdf.

[43] The fiscal commission proposes to increase the gasoline tax so that highway transportation can be fully funded by fuel taxes via the trust fund.

[44] Congressional Budget Office, *Reducing the Deficit: Spending and Revenue Options*, March 2011, http://www.cbo.gov/ftpdocs/120xx/doc12085/03-10-ReducingTheDeficit.pdf.

Plan	Provision
House Republican Budget Plan	Adopts security proposals in FY2012 budget to hold defense spending growth near inflation.
President's Framework	Reductions to hold defense spending growth close to inflation.
Galston-MacGuineas Plan	Specific cuts (weapons, military pay and TRICARE, contracting, R&D), war surtax.
Debt Reduction Task Force (Domenici-Rivlin)	Freezes for five years, then grows with GDP.
Gang of Six	Discretionary caps for 10 years, Budget Committee will create proposals to extend.

Source: The Committee for a Responsible Federal Budget, Deficit Reduction Comparison Tool. http://crfb.org/ compare/index.php?id=01, and the various plans cited in footnotes 40 and 41.

Table 16. Nondefense Discretionary Spending in Various Plans

Plan	Provision
CBO Projection	Grows with inflation.
Committee For a Responsible Federal Budget Projection	Cuts in 2011, grows with inflation.
Fiscal Commission	Spending at 2008 levels by 2013; grows at half the rate of inflation.
House Republican Budget Plan	Cuts non-security to FY2006 levels in FY2012, freezes for five years, then grows with inflation.
President's Framework	Consistent with Fiscal Commission.
Galston-MacGuineas Plan	Freezes for three years, then grows with inflation.
Debt Reduction Task Force (Domenici-Rivlin)	Freezes for four years, then grows with GDP.
Gang of Six	Discretionary caps for 10 years, instructs committees to identify specific savings.

Source: The Committee for a Responsible Federal Budget, Deficit Reduction Comparison Tool. http://crfb.org/ compare/index.php?id=01, and the various plans cited in footnotes 40 and 41.

Are Social Security and Medicare Trust Funds to be Preserved?

Since its inception in the 1930s, Social Security has been financed through a trust fund mechanism in which benefits were financed from payroll tax contributions. Payroll taxes are imposed at a flat rate, with a cap on income covered that is indexed to wages. Because of increasing disparities in income this ceiling falls lower in the income distribution than it has in the past. Benefits, while linked to contributions, are progressive in that the replacement rate for wages falls as wages rise.

Because of the link between wages and benefits, Social Security benefits were viewed by many as much like a pension, with income in retirement earned through contributions. There was a link between contributions and benefits, although it was not precise and, since the trust fund did not accumulate retirement contributions in the same way as a pension plan (but rather paid most benefits out of current contributions), the trust fund's financing was affected by demographics. Currently, the trust fund is spending more in benefits than it collects in payroll taxes and using interest earnings to fill the gap. (Note that the assets held by the trust fund are effectively borrowed by the rest of the government but are separate from the outstanding debt of the federal government held by the public.)

Benefits, as shown above, are growing faster than payroll taxes. As a result, under current policy the Social Security trust fund will eventually begin to use its assets and will become insolvent by 2036, at which point it will have income sufficient to pay about three-fourths of benefits.[45] Moreover, if a position is taken that taxes cannot be increased (as discussed below) or that payroll taxes are not to be increased, then either the close link between payroll contributions and earnings will have to be abandoned or the burden of restoring solvency will fall on cutting benefits.[46]

As shown in **Table 17**, some of the plans have specific proposals to cut benefits and raise taxes (generally by adjusting the payroll cap). These proposals tend to be similar in some respects in the types of revisions proposed. (Specific proposals for revision can also be found in the CBO budget options document.)[47]

Table 17. Social Security Provisions in Budget Plans

Plan	Provision
CBO Projection	Grows as projected by population.
Committee For a Responsible Federal Budget Projection	Same as CBO projection.
Fiscal Commission	Slows benefit growth for high and medium income, increases retirement age, indexes COLAs (cost of living adjustments) to chained CPI, includes new state and local workers, after 2020, increases payroll cap; creates new minimum and old age benefits.
House Republican Budget Plan	No revisions, process to put forward plan to deal with solvency.
President's Framework	No revisions, calls for reform without privatization or cuts for current beneficiaries to provide long term solvency.
Galston-MacGuineas Plan	Slows benefit growth for high and medium income, increases retirement ages, indexes COLAs to chained CPI, includes new state and local workers, creates new minimum and old age benefits, mandatory add-on accounts, reduces and makes payroll tax more progressive, revenues from energy tax.
Debt Reduction Task Force (Domenici-Rivlin)	Slows benefit growth for high income, indexes benefits for longevity, indexes COLAs to chained CPI, includes new state and local workers, creates new minimum and old age benefits, reduces and makes payroll tax more progressive, increases payroll cap, broadens payroll base to cover health and other employer benefits.
Gang of Six	Indexes COLAs to chained CPI, creates new minimum benefit, instructs Congress to enact reform to ensure 75-year solvency.

Source: The Committee for a Responsible Federal Budget, Deficit Reduction Comparison Tool. http://crfb.org/compare/index.php?id=01, and the various plans cited in footnotes 40 and 41.

---

[45] See CRS Report RL33514, *Social Security: What Would Happen If the Trust Funds Ran Out?*, by Christine Scott.

[46] See CRS Report RL32747, *The Economic Implications of the Long-Term Federal Budget Outlook*, by Marc Labonte.

[47] Congressional Budget Office, *Budget Options, Reducing the Deficit: Spending and Revenue Options*, March 2011, http://www.cbo.gov/ftpdocs/120xx/doc12085/03-10-ReducingTheDeficit.pdf.

Some of the proposals do not directly address Social Security revisions but rather provide instructions for a program to make the trust fund solvent. In general, therefore, there seems to be an intention to preserve the structure of the Social Security program.

The Medicare hospital insurance trust fund has been affected over time (as has Medicare in general) by demographics but, more importantly, the growth in expenditures per capita due to technical advances and cultural expectations. As shown in **Table 18**, the plans have specific suggestions for health (Medicare, Medicaid, and the new health mandates), although in some cases they include instructions to find savings in the future. There is no specific reference to trust funds and no payroll tax revenues raised for the Medicare hospital insurance trust fund.

Table 18. Health Spending Provisions in the Budget Plans

Plan	Provision
CBO Projection	Grows as projected by population and health costs.
Committee For a Responsible Federal Budget Projection	Same as CBO projection, except waives cuts to Medicare for physicians ("doc fix") which results in additional spending compared to the CBO baseline.
Fiscal Commission	Reforms "doc fix" reforms or repeals CLASS Act (voluntary long term care insurance), increases Medicare cost sharing, tort reform, changes provider payments, increases drug rebates, long term budget to limit growth after 2020 to GDP plus 1%.
House Republican Budget Plan	Assumes doc fixes are offset; repeals most health care reform (while retaining Medicare savings), tort reform, converts Medicaid into a block grant to grow with inflation and population, changes Medicare to a voucher after 2025 to grow per beneficiary with inflation.
President's Framework	Continues "doc fix," strengthens independent payment advisory board (IPAB) to address costs and limit Medicare growth to GDP plus 0.5% per beneficiary, proposes Medicaid savings by standardizing benefits.
Galston-MacGuineas Plan	Creates health budget, reduces new health insurance subsidies in 2010 legislation, tort reform, increases Medicare cost sharing, strengthens IPAB, indexes Medicare eligibility to longevity.
Debt Reduction Task Force (Domenici-Rivlin)	Continues "doc fixes," creates Medicare voucher in 2018 with growth per beneficiary at GDP plus 1%, keeping regular Medicare as a default but with premium increases, reduces Medicaid growth by 15% after 2018, tort reform, increases Medicare premiums from 25% of cost to 35%, increases drug rebates.
Gang of Six	Reform doc fix, repeal CLASS act, requires $202 billion in health care savings, tort reform, health care spending target after 2020 of GDP plus 1%, action by Congress and President if not met.

Source: The Committee for a Responsible Federal Budget, Deficit Reduction Comparison Tool. http://crfb.org/compare/index.php?id=01, and the various plans cited in footnotes 40 and 41.

Note: CBO scores the "doc fix" from over $100 billion to upwards of $300 billion over 10 years, depending on the option selected, http://cbo.gov/ftpdocs/122xx/doc12240/SGR_Menu_2011.pdf.

Can Long-Run Budget Issues be Addressed by Keeping Tax Levels and the Size of Government at FY2007 Levels?

Most of the proposals, as seen in **Table 14**, envision some increase in taxes as a percentage of output compared with FY2007, a normal year but with the Bush tax cuts in effect when taxes were 18.5% of output. One plan sets the level at 18% but the others set the tax revenue at around the peak level of taxes in history (19.5% in FY2001) or higher.

One philosophy behind the view of keeping revenues fixed relative to GDP, held by some, is that government spending takes away from private choices and creates inefficiency and that taxes impose distortions and inhibit economic activity. (This view depends on strong assumptions about benefits generated by federal spending). By limiting revenues available, the scope of the government will be constrained.

An argument is sometimes made that tax increases would inhibit economic activity so much that revenues will decline rather than rise. Empirical evidence does not generally support this view, however.[48]

If revenues are limited, significant pressure would be placed on major entitlements. For example, in **Table 13**, which may represent a more realistic picture of current programs, with revenues at 18.4% of GDP and the total of Social Security and health spending at 16.5% in 2035, only 1.9% is left for everything else with a balanced primary budget. Defense, nondefense discretionary, and other mandatory programs amount to 8.5% of GDP in 2035. Thus, it would appear that major reductions in Social Security and health spending would be required to constrain tax levels at current percentages of GDP.

The Republican Budget Committee plan, the plan which sets the tax level at 18%, sets spending at 20% in 2020, fully four percentage points below the CBO baseline (at 24) and inclusive of interest payments. How does it accomplish this?

Compared with the CBO baseline, it cuts spending by $5.8 trillion in the first 10 years. The discretionary spending cuts are large ($2.8 trillion), especially for nondefense, compared with other proposals. For nondefense spending, cuts by 2021 are 34% of the CBO baseline, which is itself low by historical measures.[49]

The second largest major change within the first 10 years, $1.4 trillion, is to repeal parts of the health care legislation that imposed costs (while retaining other cost reducing provisions).[50] The plan converts Medicaid payments to the states to a block grant which reduces spending by $0.8

---

[48] See CRS Report RL33672, *Revenue Feedback from the 2001-2004 Tax Cuts*, by Jane G. Gravelle, which suggests that the effects of the tax cuts on economic activity and the tax base would reduce the revenue loss by less than 10% and these effects would be more than offset by crowding out of private investment and increases in interest payments due to higher debt. CRS Report RL31949, *Issues in Dynamic Revenue Estimating*, by Jane G. Gravelle has a general overview of the empirical evidence on labor supply and savings. CRS Report R41743, *International Corporate Tax Rate Comparisons and Policy Implications*, by Jane G. Gravelle specifically examines a corporate rate reduction and finds similar small effects.

[49] See http://budget.house.gov/UploadedFiles/SummaryTables.pdf.

[50] See CRS Report R41196, *Medicare Provisions in the Patient Protection and Affordable Care Act (PPACA): Summary and Timeline*, coordinated by Patricia A. Davis, for additional information.

---

billion over 10 years, or 35% in 2022 according to CBO.[51] The remainder includes $0.7 trillion, from other spending, which includes, as shown in **Table 19**, a block grant for food support (SNAP), as well as other mandatory spending changes. Interest payments also fall. For Medicaid, either the benefits of the programs would have to decline or the states would have to shoulder a larger share of the financial burden.

Significant changes would be made after 2021, primarily by converting Medicare to a voucher system (required for those under 55 in 2011), which would then grow at the inflation rate. In addition, discretionary spending would continue to grow at inflation, so that it would continually decline as a percentage of output (the CBO long-run standard baseline assumes this spending will grow with output after FY2021). Essentially, this plan, in order to constrain the deficit and debt without raising taxes, converts major entitlements into fixed payments that are constrained to grow with inflation.

Although this plan and its approach are illustrative, it is suggestive of what would likely be necessary to hold the size of government and tax revenues fixed: major changes to government programs for health care and other entitlements.

Table 19. Other Mandatory Spending in Budget Plans

Plan	Provision
CBO Projection	Grows as projected.
Committee For a Responsible Federal Budget Projection	Same as CBO projection.
Fiscal Commission	Indexes using chained CPI, reforms military and civilian federal retirement, reduces farm subsidies, student loan subsidies, others.
House Republican Budget Plan	Reduces and provides block grant for supplemental nutritional assistance (SNAP) to grow with inflation and eligibility, reforms civil service retirement, reduces farm subsidies, student loan subsidies.
President's Framework	Mandatory savings targets, builds on FY2012 budget, reduces farm subsidies, student loan subsidies, others.
Galston-MacGuineas Plan	Indexes using chained CPI, phases out farm subsidies to replace with catastrophic insurance, others.
Debt Reduction Task Force (Domenici-Rivlin)	Indexes using chained CPI, reforms military and civil service retirement, reduces farm subsidies, others.
Gang of Six	$11 billion in agricultural savings (protects food stamps), indexes with chained CPI, more effective unemployment insurance triggers, sells property, reduces waste, fraud and abuse, various others.

Source: The Committee for a Responsible Federal Budget, Deficit Reduction Comparison Tool. http://crfb.org/compare/index.php?id=01, and the various plans cited in footnotes 40 and 41.

---

[51] CBO letter to Paul Ryan, chairman of the House Budget Committee, http://www.cbo.gov/ftpdocs/121xx/doc12128/04-05-Ryan_Letter.pdf.

What Would be Required to Protect Entitlements? A Review of Tax Options

To examine the other side of this coin, consider what would be required to protect entitlements. Protecting entitlements reflects a view that government should maintain its social safety net for lower income persons and programs for the elderly, including provisions for health care, important components of maintaining a reasonable standard of living.

Note that with respect to Social Security, sizeable surplus revenues have already been paid to support the payment of future benefits. Medicare HI also has accumulated surpluses that will maintain benefits for some years forward. Nevertheless, neither of these plans are sustainable in their current formulations and the shortfall in revenues relative to payments contributes to the overall deficit.

Most of the proposals already envision some increase in taxes (see **Table 20** for details) along with cuts in benefits, but also cut back on entitlements. Taxes would likely be required to rise significantly more to maintain the current level of entitlement programs. These effects can be seen by examining the different scenarios in **Table 12**, **Table 13**, and **Table 14**. In **Table 13**, taxes are held at current levels and spending rises at the higher rates under the CBO alternative baseline, with a resulting deficit of 7.5% of output in FY2021 and 15.5% of output in FY2035. Consider the lower amount of spending from the CBO baseline compared with holding taxes at current levels from the CFRB projections in **Table 14**, in which the deficit is 5.5%. As noted in the previous section, it is unlikely that cuts to discretionary and other non-entitlement spending alone would suffice to close the deficit to a sustainable level. Therefore, it is realistic to expect that taxes will rise in order to restore the path of future deficits to sustainability.

Table 20. Tax Expenditures and Tax Revisions in the Budget Plans

Plan	Provision
CBO Projection	Grows as projected.
Committee For a Responsible Federal Budget Projection	Permanent extension of 2001/2003/2010 tax cuts, and AMT patch; continues estate tax rules effective in 2011-2012.
Fiscal Commission	Calls for comprehensive reform that eliminates or revises most tax expenditures, eliminates AMT, three individual income tax rates, top rates for individual and corporate income tax between 23% and 27%, illustrative reforms (changing mortgage interest and charitable deductions to credits, phases out health exclusions, eliminates most other tax expenditures). Eliminates all tax expenditures but allows them to be added back by raising rates, assumes 2001/2003 tax cuts for those under $250,000 extended, indexes using chained CPI, moves to corporate territorial tax, increases gas tax by 15 cents per gallon to finance highway spending.
House Republican Budget Plan	2001/2003 tax cuts made permanent, revenue neutral tax reform to lower top income tax rates to 25%, corporate tax reform.
President's Framework	Supports Fiscal Commission reform, 2001/2003 tax cuts for those under $250,000 extended, revenue neutral corporate tax reform.

Plan	Provision
Galston-MacGuineas Plan	Reduces tax expenditures by 10% with half for rate reduction and half additional revenues. Specific suggestions: limit mortgage interest, phase out state and local tax deductions, replace health exclusions with credit, consolidate educational savings plans. Indexes using chained CPI, makes 2001-2003 tax cuts for those with income under $250,000 permanent, carbon tax (some used to reduce payroll tax), revenue neutral corporate tax reform.
Debt Reduction Task Force (Domenici-Rivlin)	Eliminate tax expenditures, including phase out of health exclusion, provides revised low income earnings credit and uniform child credit, preserves 2001/2003 tax cuts for those with income under $250,000, two tax rates at 15% and 27%, uses chained CPI to index, taxes alcohol and sweetened beverages, adds value added tax at 6.5%, taxes capital gains and dividends at ordinary rates.
Gang of Six	Reforms tax expenditures for health, charitable giving, homeownership and retirement, retains low income worker benefits and EITC, instructs Finance Committee to provide reform to lower rates and broaden base, three bracket 8-12%, 14-22%, 23-29%, repeals AMT, raises $1 trillion over 10 years plus additional $133 billion for highways, single corporate rate between 23% and 29%, territorial system.

Source: The Committee for a Responsible Federal Budget, Deficit Reduction Comparison Tool. http://crfb.org/compare/index.php?id=01, and the various plans cited in footnotes 40 and 41.

Justifications for Maintaining Entitlements

Is there a justification for increasing the size of government to continue the present Social Security and health benefit payments? It is useful to consider separately Social Security, whose issues arise from demographics, and health care, which arises from a combination of demographics and health care costs?

Social Security benefits are expected to rise from the current 4.8% of output to 6.1% in FY2035. However, beyond that point, the costs remain about the same, falling slightly as the baby boom generation begins to die and then rising as longevity increases. The problem with Social Security funding did not arise from the baby boom; it arose from the increase in life span whose pressures on the system were masked for a time with the growth in the labor force (both from the baby boom and entry of women into the labor force). Unlike health care, Social Security benefits are not expected to grow continuously but actually settle down so that benefits and costs are relatively constant (benefits slightly over 6% and revenues about 5% of GDP).[52] There are, therefore, a range of tax increases, as well as benefit cuts, that could bring the program into permanent balance.[53]

A CRS study of Social Security suggests that there are important justifications arising from market failure[54] and also, that there is a rationale, based on life cycle considerations, for making

---

[52] See CBO *Social Security Policy Options* for data and options, http://www.cbo.gov/doc.cfm?index=11580.

[53] Ibid.

[54] CRS Report RL31498, *Social Security Reform: Economic Issues*, by Jane G. Gravelle and Marc Labonte. Market failures include imperfect life annuities that arise from adverse selection for private retirement plans (because those who expect to live a long time and have private information about this likelihood will be more likely to purchase (continued...)

most of the adjustment in the imbalance through higher taxes rather than lower benefits.[55] Another option, which affects both taxes and benefits, is to increase the retirement age, although increases put pressure on the disability insurance program, since some individuals will find it more difficult to work longer. Thus, there are justifications for addressing more of the long run insolvency of the Social Security program through tax increases rather than benefit reductions.

This assessment considers outcomes in the steady state. There is also an issue of which generation bears the burden during the transition. The more the system relies on tax increases as opposed to benefit cuts in the short and medium term, the more the burden is shifted to younger generations.

Similar life cycle arguments could be applied to any program for the elderly to the extent it is increasing in cost because of longevity, including Medicare and nursing home costs under Medicaid. These programs are financed by a combination of payroll taxes and general revenues but most of these taxes would be collected during most individuals' working years.

Cost increases for health care are a different matter, in part because they seem to be growing continuously and in part because there are different ways to view them. To the extent that costs reflect better medical care that extends and improves the quality of life, spending more money on health care may appropriately reflect preferences of individuals, whose higher incomes permit them to spend more of their resources in this area. However, to the extent that rising medical costs reflect serious inefficiencies in the system arising from failure to allocate resources by price and causing patients and their physicians to consume large and inefficient amounts of health care, then increased benefits may not be justified.

Revenue Raising Options

If benefits are to be largely maintained, and since it is relatively clear that cutting other forms of spending will probably not be adequate for their financing, what are the tax options? Basically those options, some of which are discussed in a number of the budget proposals, are higher rates (including allowing the Bush tax cuts to expire), broadening the income tax base through reductions in tax expenditures, increasing other taxes (such as payroll and excise taxes), and introducing new taxes (such as a carbon tax).[56]

(...continued)

annuities), moral hazard (if the government commits to support low income individuals, individuals may not save for retirement and rely on poverty programs to support them in old age), and incomplete markets (inability to contract for risk-sharing across generations). In addition, limits on information, uncertainty, and myopia make it difficult for individuals to make optimal choices about saving for retirement on their own.

[55] The following quote from the report (p.19) states: "If individuals want to smooth the effects of reform over their lifetimes after reform is completed and adjusted to, they might prefer a roughly proportional effect on their standard of living. Since Social Security benefits are a larger fraction of retirement income than Social Security taxes are of workers' income, it could be argued that much of the adjustment might be made in tax increases. As an illustration, consider a case with a 10% contribution during a working period of 45 years, to finance an annuity for a retirement span of 10 years. Assume a 6% rate of return and a 2% growth in wages. If the retirement span doubled to 20 years, one could either increase the contribution by 55% or decrease the annual annuity by 35%. Suppose, however, one desired a proportional decrease in income for all years. To accomplish that would require a tax increase of about 47% and an annuity decrease of 4.7%—most of the adjustment (85%) would come on the tax side. The share allocated to taxes would still be significant if the Social Security annuity represented only part of retirement income. For example, the average share of retirement income from Social Security is 51% for singles and 37% for married couples. With these shares, the tax adjustment would be between about two-thirds and about three-fourths of the total adjustment."

[56] For additional discussion of revenue options, see CRS Report R41641, *Reducing the Budget Deficit: Tax Policy* (continued...)

Rates can easily be varied and many of the proposals include allowing the Bush tax cuts, especially for high income taxpayers, to expire. These tax cuts primarily arise from rate reductions. The barriers for rate increases might be viewed as largely political rather than technical and top tax rates in the past have been much higher than they are today. Allowing the temporary tax provisions to expire and including real bracket creep is reflected in the difference between the CBO standard and alternative baselines, and accounts for 2.4% of GDP.

Although tax expenditures have received much attention and are included in budget proposals, policy makers face significant political and technical barriers to implementing changes. Some tax expenditures are technically difficult to eliminate (especially employer fringe benefits), some are valued as part of the social safety net (such as the earned income credit or exclusion of transfers), some are desirable for other reasons, and some are so politically popular (e.g., the home mortgage interest deduction) that eliminating them or scaling them back could be difficult.[57]

For example, considering technical challenges alone, the largest individual tax expenditure is the exclusion of employer health insurance, which accounts for 11% of the total revenue foregone. As discussed during the health reform debate, however, there are many difficulties in fairly designing an inclusion, since the value of insurance varies, for example, with the age of the employee and other characteristics. If not allowed to vary by age, young employees who work for firms with higher average employee ages will be imputed more income than employees working for firms with younger employees. Potentially more serious imputation problems arise with the third largest tax expenditure (the exclusion of pension contributions and earnings), which accounts for 9% of the total, because of defined benefit pension plans whose benefits are difficult to allocate because they ultimately depend on future work history with the firm.

At the same time, many of the proposals discussed in **Table 20** also envision using elimination of tax expenditures to lower rates. If used only for revenue purposes, significant progress towards reducing the deficit might be made. One study, for example, suggests that a more realistic appraisal of tax expenditure options, taking into account technical barriers, political barriers, and justification for some provisions, would increase income tax revenues by about 15%.[58] In the CBO alternative baseline, income tax revenues would be about 10.6% in FY2021, suggesting increased revenues of 1.6% of GDP. This increase is about two-thirds of the difference in revenues between the regular and alternative CBO baselines, which reflect the Bush tax cuts,

---

(...continued)

Options, by Molly F. Sherlock.

[57] For a discussion of these issues, both for individuals and corporations, see Jane G. Gravelle, "Practical Tax Reform for a More Efficient Income Tax," *Virginia Tax Review*, vol. 30, no. 2, fall, 2010, pp. 389-406.

[58] Ibid. Individual income tax expenditures included lower dollar caps on mortgage interest deductions, disallowing mortgage interest deductions for vacation homes and home equity loans, ceilings on employer deductions for health insurance/care plans, a percentage of income cap for state and local taxes, along with disallowing personal property and sales taxes, taxing dividends at ordinary rates and taxing capital gains at higher rates, treating carried interest as ordinary income, including capital gains preferences in the AMI, disallowing like-kind exchanges, disallowing capital gains treatment for timber, coal and iron ore, repealing cafeteria plans, a percentage of income floor for charitable contributions, reducing deductions for gifts of appreciated property to basis, eliminating the charitable IRA rollover, taxing Social Security benefits as pensions, substituting a 25% credit for tax exempt bond exclusion, taxing inside buildup on insurance plans currently, and repealing IRAs for those covered by employer plans. This proposal would liberalize the capital gains exclusion for gain on owner occupied housing. Many of these provisions are also included in CBO budget options, *Reducing the Deficit: Spending and Revenue Options*, http://www.cbo.gov/ftpdocs/120xx/ doc12085/03-10-ReducingTheDeficit.pdf.

---

other temporary provisions, and some real bracket creep (growth in revenues because real income are rising).

Two other types of taxes that might be altered are the payroll tax and excise taxes. For example, some proposals have included a provision for raising or eliminating the cap on earnings for payroll taxes. Other options include raising rates, and expanding the base to include fringe benefits (such as pension contributions and health care). (Imputing income, however, as noted above, may be problematic.) A number of options could significantly extend solvency to the Social Security trust fund.[59] Revenue could also be raised by taxing Social Security benefits in the same way as pensions, and this revenue, although considered as part of tax expenditures, could be designated to finance Social Security benefits.

Proposals have also included increases in gasoline taxes to provide additional funding for highways, and increases in alcohol taxes, whose real value has been declining since 1991, and would be an estimated 60% higher if they had been indexed to inflation since then.

Finally, there are options for additional types of taxes. Three new tax sources which have been included in the proposals are value added taxes, carbon taxes (revenue could also be collected through an auction of carbon rights through a cap and trade system), and taxes on sugar-sweetened beverages. Both value added taxes and carbon taxes could raise significant amounts of additional revenues.

These revenue sources differ in the incentives they create and also in their progressivity. Because income taxes tend to fall more heavily than other taxes on high-income individuals, and tax expenditures tend to benefit higher income individuals, these changes would likely add to the progressivity of the system. Changes in payroll rates would tend to be proportional and affect higher income individuals less, although raising the cap would concentrate the effect on higher income workers. Flat rate consumption taxes, including value added taxes, carbon taxes and specific excise taxes (such as those on gasoline, alcohol and sugared beverages) tend to be regressive. A combination of changes could, however, achieve approximately the same distribution as current revenues.

Effects on State and Local Governments

Some of the proposals would address the budget deficit by reducing transfers to state and local governments. Since the details of discretionary spending (other than caps and limits) are not generally spelled out, some of this reduction could reduce transfers to state and local governments in areas such as education, transportation, and community development. In addition, many entitlements, both for health and income security, are administered by the state and local governments with federal transfers. One of the largest of these programs is Medicaid which the House Republican Budget proposal restricts to a block grant that grows at population rates plus inflation rates. As noted above, federal transfers to state and local governments are 2.8% of output, and constitute 21% of the receipts of these governments. State and local governments also benefit from tax expenditures that allow itemized deductions for state and local taxes and exclusions for interest on state and local bonds. Depending on how these governments respond,

---

[59] Congressional Budget Office, *Social Security Policy Options*, July 2010, http://www.cbo.gov/ftpdocs/115xx/doc11580/07-01-SSOptions_forWeb.pdf.

restrictions that affect state and local transfers could largely shift the burden of spending from federal to subnational governments.

Author Contact Information

Jane G. Gravelle
Senior Specialist in Economic Policy
jgravelle@crs.loc.gov, 7-7829

www.ingramcontent.com/pod-product-compliance
Lightning Source LLC
Chambersburg PA
CBHW080631290526
45790CB00007B/3019